Dreams, Vietnam

Marc Levy

Winter Street Press
Salem, MA 01970

Dreams, Vietnam

ISBN: 978-0-692-77637-7

First Edition

Front cover: Pederson's bunker on LZ Francis. Tay Ninh, Vietnam, 1970. Photo: author's collection

ACKNOWLEDGMENTS

I would like to thank the following persons: Bruce Weigl and Martha Collins provided invaluable critiques and advice. Erin McManus, Richard Levine and Susan Moger proof read the manuscript. Bill Domhoff for his work and support.

FOREWARD

As far as I know, this is the first instance in which a large number of dreams from a war veteran suffering from PTSD has been made available in print to everyone. As such, this remarkable dream journal is a gift to all of us for what it conveys about the horrors of war and the agony of PTSD. Its appearance is also a testament to Marc Levy's emotional strength and his determination to persevere in the face of the debilitating effects of PTSD, and to his decision to speak out in ways that will make it possible for more people to comprehend what it is like to live with PTSD. I hope his dream journal will bring feelings of emotional recognition to the PTSD sufferers who read it, as well as new insights and understanding for everyone.

This dream journal is also a gift for those of us who study dreams. Systematic studies of about two dozen dream journals kept by everyday people for their own highly varied reasons led to the unexpected discovery that people's dreams are generally consistent in their content over months, years, and even decades. That's something we might never have learned using our usual methods of collecting a few dreams from many different people through awakenings in sleep-and-dream laboratories and in middle school, high school, and university classrooms.

In addition, findings from studies of about a dozen dream journals reveal that people's dream lives are by and large continuous with their waking thoughts and concerns. For example, these studies show that the frequency with which people dream about a person or activity indicates the intensity of their concerns (whether positive or negative) with that person or activity in waking life. These conclusions derive from developing inferences based on quantitative studies of a dream journal's contents without knowing anything about the dreamer. Then feedback from the dreamer usually corroborates these inferences. When the same questions can be asked independently of close friends of the dreamer, they usually agree with the dreamer, which provides evidence from more detached but highly knowledgeable observers.

Based on these and other studies, it can be tentatively concluded that a great many of our dreams dramatize our major personal concerns, and that certainly proves to be the case in Marc Levy's journal as well. Dreams give us a portrait of how we view the important people and activities in our waking life. They most closely resemble plays in waking life because they include characters, settings, social interactions, activities, and emotions. They literally embody our thoughts because the feelings and activities in a dream seem so vivid and real while they are happening. Sometimes it is difficult to believe the experience was "only a dream" when we awaken from a particularly unusual or frightening dream. As a famous psychologist, Havelock Ellis, said over one hundred years ago, "Dreams are real while they last. Can we say more of life."

Since it might seem implausible to claim that dream journals are highly useful to scientists, who usually (and rightly) place great emphasis on experiments or close naturalistic observations, let me add that those usual methods are not possible to use in studying dreams. Studies long ago showed we can't make dreams happen, even in a sleep lab, and of course we can't observe them while they are happening. So all we ever have is the dreamer's report of a memory of an experience that happened during sleep. In the case of dream journals, they have the great virtue that those who keep them wrote very detailed and candid accounts because it was not their intention to show them to others. The details are needed so they recall the dream better when they reread it later. In addition, their dream recall is usually better to begin with than it is for most people, who remember two or three dreams a week at best, and they often become even better dream recallers as they pay more attention to their dreams. And to the degree that scientists ever see such journals, it is because those who keep them later learn through stories in the media that such journals are of interest to dream researchers.

At this point let me add that several of the dream journals from which I drew the new and unexpected conclusions about consistency and continuity in people's dream lives can be found at dreambank.net, which also contains many dream journals that have not been studied in detail. Dreambank.net also includes dream reports collected from groups of people in sleep-and-dream labs as well as in classrooms. There are about 20,000 dream reports in English and another 6,000 in German. Several researchers have made use of various subsets of these dream reports, as have a few artists and writers, as well as people from all walks of life who want to examine dreams out of their own curiosity.

Let me further add that it is to the good fortune of dream researchers that Marc Levy offered his dream journal for inclusion on dreambank.net, which I view as a treasure for future studies. He also took the time in 2015 to write down 32 dreams he remembered over a three-week period, which makes it possible to do interesting comparisons with his earlier dream journal. Moreover, the fact that he reports so much detail on his life, thoughts, and writings on his web site Medic in the Green Time.com makes his original dream journal and the follow-up 2015 journal all the more valuable for studies of the relationship between dreams and waking cognition and emotion.

I therefore salute and express my gratitude to him for sharing his dream journal in this book and on dreambank.net. I also consider it an honor to be asked to write this foreword to what I think is an invaluable contribution to future studies of PTSD and the incredibly frightening dreams that are one of its most dreaded symptoms I hope for the day when teams of psychologists and neuroscientists focus some of their neuroimaging studies on patients who have kept dream journals, perhaps beginning with Marc Levy himself, who has dealt with PTSD with courage, insight, and perseverance for over 45 years. As he explained to me via email when I asked him about his sleeping circumstances, he slept with a loaded twenty-five caliber automatic pistol under his pillow from 1972 to 1974, kept a meat cleaver under his pillow between 1983 and 1989, and slept with a machete next to him from 1997 to 2000. He still sleeps on a futon placed directly on the floor and cannot sleep with his back to the bedroom door or with the door open.

There could be no better starting point for developing a neurocognitive theory of dreaming that might help to reduce human suffering than the dream journal you are about to read.

G. William Domhoff
Distinguished Professor Emeritus and Research Professor
University of California, Santa Cruz
http://www2.ucsc.edu/dreams/About/bill.html

March 30, 2016

PREFACE

1970 was a comparatively easy year for Delta 1/7 First Cavalry Division in Vietnam. Three weeks a month were spent on jungle patrol. Once a month we pulled guard on remote fire bases. Our area of operation included: Bien Hoa, Phuc Binh, Phuc Vinh, An Loc, Loc Ninh, Quan Loi, Song Be, Tay Ninh, and Bu Dop There were no pitched battles. Heavy losses were uncommon. The company saw most of its action, and took most of its casualties during the Cambodia invasion, where Delta helped defend LZ Ranch when it was overrun.

Nine months after returning from Vietnam, and while still on active duty at Fort Devens, I began recording my war nightmares, though the first entry occurred during combat. The journal contains 102 entries; not all nightmares were recorded.

The original entries for 30 May and 25 July 81, long lost, are partially restored. Although war dreams continued from 1981 to 1999, only one entry was made. I resumed the journal in 1999. I ended it in 2003. A final entry was made in 2008.

The entries are dated by day, month and year and have been edited for clarity. Multiple dreams on the same date are separated by a double space. There are occasional footnotes.

Many of the persons identified in the dreams were in my platoon. For example, Lt. Steve Sharp, of Bloomington, Indiana, was third platoons leader. Elsewhere, Robert Misurel was a long time friend from Newark, NJ. Peter Ahr, a friend for many years, was the Dean of Students at Seton

Hall University, where I met John Kraft and David Boyle. Jamie Harter is a physician, met while working in New Zealand in 1994-1995. The late George Dickerson, a writer and actor, was a close friend. Bao Ninh, a Vietnamese veteran, is the author of the acclaimed novel *The Sorrow of War*. We met in Boston in 1998. The late Gloria Emerson was a New York Times war correspondent and novelist. We met in Boston in 2000, where I also met the poet Marilyn Nelson in 2001.

Marc Levy
Salem, MA 2016

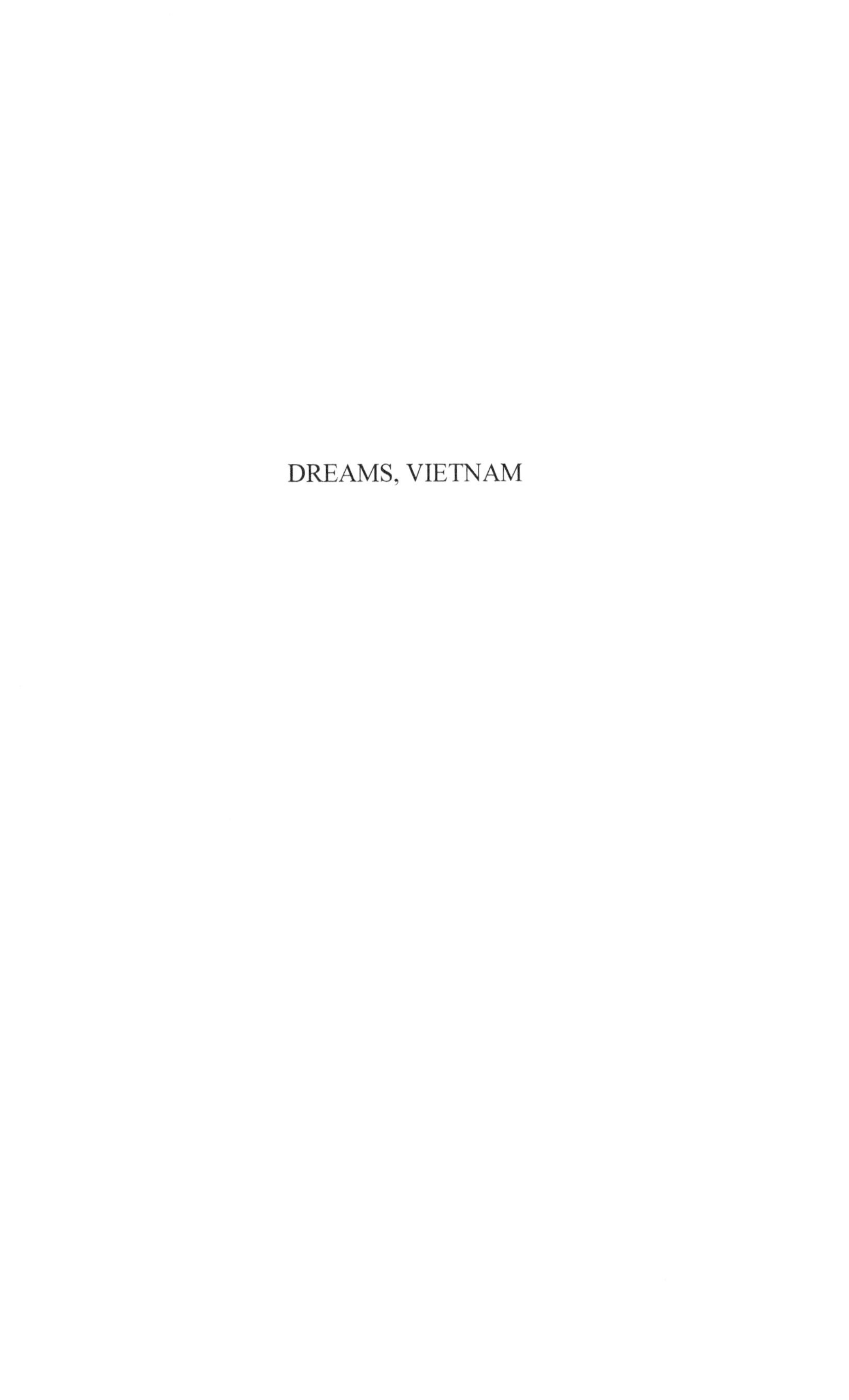

DREAMS, VIETNAM

Patrols, jungle, ambush, monsoon. I was the medic.
These are my dreams.

D 1/7 First Cavalry Division was alleged to be the last unit to leave Cambodia when the invasion ended. In 1999, Lt. Steve Sharp recalled the unit being followed by NVA. On the night before re-crossing back to Vietnam, with ammo bandoliers slung across my chest, my M16 close at hand, and wearing my .45 pistol, I slept head to foot with squad leader Jerry Bieck.

28 June 70

We're being overrun by sappers. They've gotten got past the trips and claymores and crawl forward.

I wake up from the dream and see a boot tread near my face. Slowly, I take my .45 from its holster, pull the hammer back, aim it. Then the moon came out and I saw the boot treads were American. It was Jerry's foot. We'd slept near each other that night. In the stillness I pointed the .45 straight up, pinched the hammer, pulled the trigger, settled the hammer back in place, re-holstered the pistol and went back to sleep. That morning, after a hard march, we left Cambodia, having been there forty-six days.

In 1998 I related the dream to Jerry Bieck. He laughed and said, "Doc, that would have put a big dent in my golf game."

30 July 71

The enemy is in the sky. We're not soldiers but school children. A voice from everywhere warns us, "Things are dropping." Seeds begin to fall. I hear the faint echo of the tubes popping[2]. There is an underground bunker but most of us run for the school bus. The mortars drop within twenty yards. The fear of death races through my mind. We crowd into the bus, scared of a hit. I shield my face with two paperback books. All at once there is a sharp explosion. I'm hit, but scream just for a moment. It's such a helpless feeling. The concussion has shattered my teeth. I'm going into shock.

---

[2] Tubes popping: the sound of enemy mortar shells popping out of the tubes that launch them.

31 August 71

We're on a firebase. In the distance a flare ignites. Someone says the intelligence reports indicate we may be attacked. I enter a bunker and search for my aid bag which is full of bandages. It's empty. I decide to look elsewhere before it's too late. I'm in a house; all of a sudden mortars drop, close and loud. I feel guilty. The house can withstand a direct hit, but I'm terrified. The shells continue falling with their distinct metallic *crackBANG*. When the attack is over, I run out. My entire platoon, all fifteen men, sit in a grotesque formation of the dead.

14 September 71

We're on a firebase. It seems more like World War II than Vietnam. I'm saying good bye to an American girl. We embrace. Her father is dressed like a Navy admiral. We begin talking. He details the need for security and mentions Crazy Frank, the grunt who played with the dead. The many soldiers present are not regular grunts. Everyone drops. We wait, expecting to be hit by machine guns. Someone signals false alarm. A black soldier stands up. He's angry, even though we've obeyed our instincts to drop at the slightest sound.

The commander and I resume talking. This time there's no mistake. I hear the tubes popping. I say to the officer, "Run for the bunkers." Everyone runs. In my mind, I count off eight seconds, the time we have to escape. The commander tries to run past me. I've completely forgotten about the girl.

The bunker seems familiar, as if from another dream. When I'm just inside the mortars begin to fall, exploding right over us. I run to a corner and huddle. I'm near an portal, though beneath it, and must look up. A shell descends with a terrific whining and hits close by. I'm knocked down by the blast, but not injured. Not far away, a .30 cal opens up. We're being overrun.

7 October 71

This time, it is not the tubes popping, but the whistling of the mortars themselves that alerts us. We run for the bunkers, which have cinder block foundations like new homes being built. There is no roof, only a few pieces of lumber overhead. It's very, very open.

The mortars begin to drop. I hear the explosions loud and clear. I anticipate a direct hit. The shelling is relentless. Someone says, "After the attack, beware. It's an old VC trick to draw out the defenders, then renew the attack." But nothing happens.

29 December 71

Robert and I seem to be part of an infantry company. We sleep in canvas tents. Then the dream unfolds as if I'm another person, watching what happens. The enemy attacks and I'm shot in the head. I'm behind a wall, but still in danger of being hit. In a fury I grab a silver object that resembles an RPG, and hurl it at the enemy. It explodes, covering everything in flames. Even the person watching the dream.

3 January 72

We're on patrol. It's not my old unit, but the feelings are the same. As usual we're spread out, three or four meters between each man. The jungle ahead becomes less thick. We can see twenty-five to thirty meters forward. Things are going too well. I anticipate an ambush. They are not the familiar pops of the AK, but with the first shots I drop to the ground. The men up front fire back, killing two. Two enemy soldiers begin to rise up and I yell to the grunts, at the same time aiming my M16 at the enemy and pulling the trigger. The gun jams. I reload another magazine and pull the trigger, but nothing happens. The grunts fire, and the attack seems over.

In the background, I hear a sharp whining recoil. It's nothing like our 105s or 155s. The number 106 flashes through my mind. The first shells fall outside our perimeter. They don't drop like mortars or explode like artillery. On impact there is a sharp thunder-clap, followed by swirling earth-like clouds of thick dust, which hug the ground. The shells drop closer. I hear the shrapnel whizzing past. Finally a shell lands almost on top of me and I imagine a large piece of steel penetrating the flesh of my back. There is no pain, but this is a death wound. The last moments are obscured by dust.

28 December 72

We are walking down a well-used trail. In the distance I see a sort of rubber plantation occupied by NVA. Just then Clopton the RTO[3] comes running past, dressed in white. He's been wounded in the arm. We form a perimeter. An enemy machine gun team walks right up to us. Everyone is too scared to open up. I peel off three short bursts and rip the gunner in half. A few minutes later, it happens again. A single enemy soldier walks up to us. I spatter him wickedly with my M16. It's a good feeling, though I'm worried about ammo.

We retreat to a large building and cluster fuck inside. It's similar to the room I'm living in now. Several grunts flop on beds and rest. I think about pulling guard twice a night. It's a wonder we get enough sleep. I want to close my eyes and doze off but fear keeps me awake. Someone guards the side door. I shift about, expecting an attack.

---

[3] RTO: radio telephone operator

21 March 73

We're on a well-used trail, the platoon is walking drag[4]. Up in front AK and 16 shots are exchanged. At first no one hits the ground. Instead we look to see what has happened. Capt. Hyslop stands over a dead VC. Suddenly the bamboo becomes a barren hilly expanse and we're surrounded by NVA. Some of them are holed up in a modern building on a ledge one hundred meters to the right. Way off I see an NVA machine gunner beading on us. I shoot him. Close by, another NVA gunner appears. I have a machine gun. We duel with bullets. An NVA on the ledge hurls a Chicom at me. I have four seconds until it explodes. I hug the earth. The grenade lands short. The first NVA gunner rolls a base ball grenade towards me. I consider my chances, grab it and hurl it far away. It explodes in the air. The machine gun duel continues. His bullets churn up dust in front of me. I fire a long burst and kill him with one shot in the chest. Then AK's open up. It's like the June ambush in Cambodia. I fear running out of ammo. Now I'm with the point man, Larry Roy. We're by a conex[5] filled with ammo. We deliberate what to do.

---

[4] drag: last in line

[5] conex: a steel cargo container

June ambush several members of third platoon were wounded after one chicom blew up the machine gun and another landed between us.

22 March 73

I'm in a strange sort of bunker. It resembles the bar in the basement of my childhood home. I'm lying on a counter top. I see sandbags and timber. The sky is overcast. Strange bombs are falling. A sharp bang follows the initial blast. I throw myself over the edge and fall to the ground. Cowering under flimsy wood I wait for a direct hit. Within seconds a large shell crashes where I had lain. Dirt clods and wood splinters rain down. It's all about luck.

The basement bar consisted of a small pine wood counter top, pine wood cabinets, and several small stools.

17 January 77

As related to Jungian therapist Ira Sharkey at Klinic am Zurichberg, Zurich, Switzerland.

Cowboys and Indians are fighting a desperate battle. One cowboy has six arrows in his back. When the dream ends the credits roll. The main actor is Redman. All the cowboys are named Redman.

Ira asked if I had any thoughts about the dream. I said we had a casualty who was shot six times during an ambush. His name was Red. Immediately I broke down sobbing. Twenty years later, a platoon member disclosed what really happened: A few weeks prior, Red had been warned to follow orders, to advance during contact. The day of the ambush, angry platoon members shot him for again failing to move up. When I got to Red, I saw that he had been shot in the arms, legs and gut. He looked at me while I bandaged his wounds, but kept silent. In fact, no one spoke. A medivac arrived and took Red away. We never heard from or mentioned him again.

-There are no entries for the next five years-

20 February 78

We're on a firebase in Cambodia. I'm not with my platoon but part of the TOC. The captain who could not read maps is the battalion commander. We gather in a large canvas tent. I want to dig in but there are no shovels. Night comes. I hear the illumination flare's metallic ping. No one knows who has called for lume. Through the thin canvas I see two figures run past. Ground attack, but I say nothing.

The NVA position themselves in old houses and begin firing their AKs. I'm with my old platoon. We converge on them. I cut down several enemy soldiers. I'm overwhelmed by the sight of two Americans fighting alongside them. One is Mike Wilson, the RTO. I fire at him but the bullets dumbly chug out of my M16. Wilson is shot by Juba, a high school friend of mine, with a long barreled forty-five. He shoots just as Wilson sprays a burst across my chest, but I'm not wounded. The fire fight ends. We go back to the tent. I see bullet holes in my ankles. The captain asks if there is anything I need. I think of saying "Yes, a medivac" but tell him we should dig in.

The next day I search for ammo but there's none to be found. I steal two grenades. I meet John Roop and Steve Melhop, two men from my platoon. During a fire fight I throw grenades, letting them cook two seconds after pulling the pin. They hiss like smoke grenades, and bounce because I throw too hard. When the grenades explode only sparks appear.

Steve Shack, a childhood friend, arrives. We go to the side of the base with a small Vietnamese compound. Steve throws a grenade into a wood school house, blowing it up. We hear the terrible screams of the children. The two of us walk down a trail. I tell him how stupid he was for making that mess. I tell him the enemy will take revenge. Shrieking children come running after us. "Come with me," I say.

"Come to me." A jeep pulls up and takes on casualties.

20 March 78

I'm like a spy, and have done something for a man in trouble. I go with another person and demand to be paid. I'm adamant. I say, "You will pay me now!" I'm given a large sum of money. I'm aware that others will try to steal it. I have to escape. I'm running. Then I'm found. The ones who seek me begin shooting. I dive behind a large machine gun and fire back. A star of David descends over this scene.

8 December 78

I'm in a hostile land. There's a war going on. With two brothers I sit in a crude rock shelter, perched on high ground, overlooking an immense river.

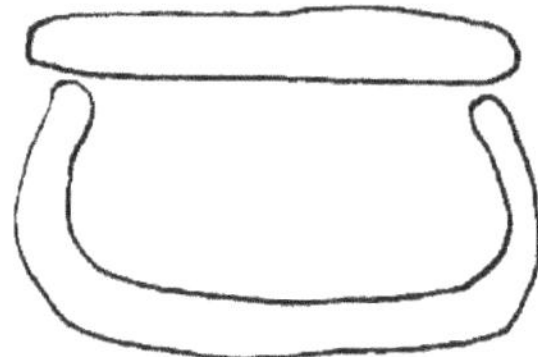

Between us there is one magazine of ammunition. Moments earlier, I let pass the chance to get more.

We anticipate an ambush. Two Chinese men on horseback trot up the hill. One dismounts and walks up to the open ports of the shelter. He has a samurai sword. I lunge my M 16 into his chest and pull the trigger. Instead of the sharp bang, the sound is muffled and dull. With his sword, the Chinaman hacks and slashes my arm but he is the one who dies.

20 July 79

I'm a soldier flying a small balsa wood plane by telepathy. It crashes to the ground and wounds a sleeping solider in the head. As I return to my living quarters I tell the incident to the soldiers following me. Two blacks become greatly excited. One takes out his pistol and wags it about. I'm shot in the thigh. I think of the dull pain that begins to throb. The blood begins to gush from my femoral artery. I wonder where I can find a tourniquet.

22 October 79

I'm in basic training. A drill sergeant upbraids me. I beat and pummel him until he is dead. I go to Vietnam. I'm with my old company but I'm not accepted. I become a loner, an outcast. Roaming about, I shoot down American helicopters. A Chinook lands. FNGs[9] exit and begin to march in single file. I shoot them but instead of bullets only water sprays out.

---

[9] FNGs: friendly new guys, replacements

30 November 79

I'm with a friend. We have traveled to a strange land. The people resemble the Pineys of the Pine Barrens in New Jersey. They are kind, friendly, they share food with us. I feel at home. They present me with many small gifts. Now I'm perched on a high ledge. A college English teacher will read a poem by David Boyle. David asks to read it himself. The poem is written in hieroglyphs. There are crows and hawks and bird tracks. As David reads I become emotional. Moments later I'm weeping.

I return to this land with my old platoon. Everything is gone, scorched; nothing remains. I load my M16 with the new and unfamiliar banana clip. We're ambushed. I squeeze off a few rounds then run for cover. I lose sight of my platoon. They patrol without me. Without their medic. I'm overcome by guilt. We link up. I'm ashamed of myself, but glad to see the men are safe. The lieutenant is stern with me. The shame passes.

6 January 80

Several men are smoking pot in a small park enclosed by a barbed wire fence. I recognize John and David from college, and Larry Johnson, a sergeant shot in Cambodia. From the corner of my eye I see the police. They run up and arrest us. Someone I don't recognize tries to escape. He vaults the fence and heads for the woods. The police send dogs after him. It seems hopeless, but he runs fast and gets away. We are herded into a jail in India. The jail has many small rooms with thick metal bars. Over and over I tell myself, "This can't be happening to me. It's only a dream." But I'm not dreaming. I'm really locked up. A jailer opens a cell and allows David to leave. The jailer offers me freedom if I will become an informer. I say to myself, "It's only a trick. Besides, I can't betray my friends." I languish in the little cell.

7 January 80

I'm led to prison. A black man in front of me kisses the jailers hand. I walk past, then turn around and do the same. The gesture is followed by submissive talk. I'm hoping that the jailer will be lenient on me. I escape. Holy chanting sounds rise from a cave. The shadows of animals run past on its walls. Now I'm flying through rock, then thick lava-like water, then water. I see a length of rope and reach for it. My head clears the water and I emerge from a beautiful lake. Still clinging to the rope, I'm one tenth my normal size. I have been hoisted up by a child, a little girl perhaps seven years old.

22 February 80

I'm in a large classroom. The teacher calls the roll. "Veterans," he says. No one answers. A second time the name is called. I yell, "Don't you know that's me, you big baboon?" Everyone laughs. Even the teacher, who resembles Dr. DeStefano[10] the plastic surgeon, breaks into a grin. The laughter turns to great applause. Everyone is smiling, applauding, cheering. These people are familiar. They're from my past. Here, they are children. The pitch grows higher. I'm born aloft by many hands and deposited at the head of the class, alongside the teacher, and four pretty girls. I'm thinking, "He is overweight, but he does not look like a baboon."

---

[10] Dr. DeStephano was consulted for injuries sustained after a 1979 assault ruled an attempted homicide.

20 June 80

I'm with my old unit in Vietnam. The order comes over the radio that we are finished with patrols. The lieutenant makes it official, and we silently begin to disband. Suddenly, a civilian, an older man in a suit, emerges from a tent. He speaks to us. "If my son can't go, no one goes." Then he shoots and kills my Jerry the RTO. I'm overwhelmed and shoot him several times. Nothing happens. Then, with an unusually long burst of automatic from my M16 I cut him down. As the others have walked off, I throw down the weapon and follow after them. I feel completely free. In high spirits Jim the machine gunner and I go to a supermarket and buy food. I'm aware that I don't have on my steel helmet. The dream is repeated. This time I do the killing with a laser beam. This time, the man I kill is Dennis, a medic from another company whom I did not like. He dies a slow agonizing death.

7 July 80

I'm in a large empty house. My brother and I are dressed like soldiers. We're hunting each other. I see him before he spots me and hit him with a burst from my M16. I walk the bullets up to him, but they make only a small BB pattern and little noise. There's little impact, little of the expected striking force, but he falls and I rush to his aid. I feel very sorry for him, for what I have done.

15 November 80

There's a war going on between the Americans and Germans, or the Russians; the battleground resembles World War I. The land between the two sides is like the no-man's land of LZ Ranch[11] in Cambodia. Each side fires artillery, adjusting for accuracy. The shells fly back and forth, falling with muffled dull thuds. Then the other side launches a ground attack, throwing hand grenades on the run. The grenades hit the ground and bounce forward. I catch one and hurl it back. Then another, then two more. The others do the same. Now I'm in hand to hand combat with a man about fifty years old. He is fat and ruddy and taunts me with a sinister look. Twisting his knife through the air he's clearly the more skilled fighter. He nicks me several times. Somehow, as my knife becomes a fork, I spear him in the throat. His eyes bulge; the gushing blood mixes with his last gurgling breath.

[11] LZ Ranch was a firebase built in Cambodia during the invasion. The gap between the base and the jungle was not wide enough and not sufficiently cleared of trees and brush. The base was overrun on 16 May 1970. Casualties were heavy

2 January 81

Having gotten past the guards, my brother and I break into an Army base. There are cases and cases of grenades stacked up. I open one box, take out a grenade, and throw it. It explodes. We see my father in the distance. He calls to us. As we walk forward, I throw missiles at him. They are like giant bullets, arching up, then falling and crashing down. We speak to him about flowers. He insists that gardening and cultivation are no different from nature. My brother and I argue against him.

The scene changes. Looking out a window I can see I'm very high off the ground. A man below reads out winning lottery numbers. Thousands of people gather. He has somehow angered them. I fall out the window but survive. Then a huge oblong metal plate tumbles down and strikes me on the head, a deathblow. I'm getting weak from loss of blood. I'm weeping. My mother tries to comfort me. In between my sobs I tell her to contact Peter. I tell her his address. I tell her to give Peter this message: "Tell David I'm sorry." Since the wound is not too bad, I suggest we go for an x-ray.

5 March 81

I'm on patrol in Vietnam with my brother and Bob Misurel. My brother wears a camouflage T-shirt. We tramp through the jungle until we reach a clearing. It's a great sloping field, like those in the Watchung Reservation in New Jersey. My brother goes on recon. Two GIs at the bottom of a hill mistake him for VC and fire at him. I signal them, but too late. I see my brother being shot. From behind, another GI shoots at my brother. At fifty meters I shoot the GI with a long burst from my M16. The bullets arc through the air like artillery shells.

Bob grabs the man I have wounded while I go to the aid of my brother. We take them both to a nearby hospital which resembles my boyhood grammar school. A doctor takes each man into the operating room.

Bob and I return to the clearing. Behind us, another medic, whom I dislike, approaches on horseback. He jeeringly announces that my brother is dead. I'm heartbroken and begin to sob and weep. Then, fueled by anger, I grab the horse by its throat and wrestle it to the ground, easing my sorrow.

Bob and I return to the hospital, crossing streets similar to the ones where I grew up. A policeman halts an oncoming car that I have waited to let pass. I have a terrible sense of grief.

12 March 81

I'm trying to squeeze into a small English sports car. When it does not stop moving I say, "Fuck you" to the driver. He returns and challenges me to a fight.

Now we're in the garage of Bob's parents. I'm full of confidence and cunning. I outmaneuver the driver, stabbing him in the back with a knife. I say, "Give up or I'll kill you." He yields and I help him outside and dress his wounds.

8 May 81

I'm in the army at Ivy Hill Park.[12] Soon we'll go out on patrol. It's getting dark, so I go out to collect fire wood. David and I are lying prone in a lake. The water is only a few inches deep. David has an explosive charge but no matches to light it. I become serious and tell him to keep his voice down. I tell him to find matches. Something is not right. The water is not deep. Suddenly we are charged from our right flank by a dozen men with fixed bayonets. They look Oriental, but at the last moment I see they are GIs. I've been the butt of a joke. Rolling on the ground, David and I howl with laughter. We begin to sing a popular song. Our harmony and rhythm are surprisingly good.

[12] Ivy Hill Park known from childhood, an 18 acre semi-wooded neighborhood park with a playground, ball fields, and tennis court.

30 May 81

I'm in Vietnam caught in a rocket attack. These are not like the devastating 122s fired at Quan Loi. They are scaled down ICBMs that whoosh in slow motion like outgoing 155s. As the missiles explode I see the hot shrapnel whirl through the air. I'm running for cover to avoid it. I dive through a window into an underground room. I've taken fragments in the sole of my boot and my right arm. More rockets fall. The sharp explosions generate flashes of light. I'm terrified but do not panic. Then I'm with my old platoon. The lieutenant says I should not be ashamed of my cowardice. I'm to be relieved or reassigned. The men act as if nothing is wrong. Their remarks only heighten my shame.

2 June 81

I'm on a small wooden dock by a lake. With a long carrot I taunt a giant snapping turtle. I hit his nose without letting him bite. Then he manages to clinch the carrot and I see the full length of his jaw and teeth. He half raises up and grabs the carrot more firmly. I'm terrified and not sure what to do. I had not realized the turtle was so big and powerful.

8 July 81

I'm in a place that resembles Vietnam selecting a hotel room that can withstand mortars and bullets.

Now I'm in a war zone, as if I've returned to Vietnam. All the buildings in the previous part of the dream are nearly destroyed. There's the chance of being attacked. Much of the landscape resembles Ivy Hill, the area where I grew up. I kill a black man with a burst from my M16. To escape, I find a train that goes from Vietnam to Thailand. I get out, careful not to be caught for desertion. A man checks my ID. He finds four stamps in my wallet given to me by my mother. He asks why I still carry them. I offer him one, leaving me three.

I return to Vietnam. It feels like the danger has increased. A feeling of death and destruction haunts me, more than contact with NVA or VC. A friend and I decide to escape by car. He drives, taking the turns too wide, with no idea where he's going. Seeing the jungle, I'm afraid we'll be ambushed.

25 July 81

I'm the leader of a small group of young people. An odd looking man walks past and makes a remark. A few moments later several bandits approach and fire their pistols. I yell "No!" but am shot in the face. I feel the huge hollow gash where the left side of my face has been blown away. It's a mortal wound, but I do not die.

I'm on a wooden raft in a lake fighting a large black man. We each have long bamboo fishing poles. We use them like adept Tai Chi push-sword players, both of us are extremely good at directing and slipping touches. He wants to snag me with the hook. Without trying, I land a blow to his head and he tumbles into the water. A small group of people on the river bank have watched him ungracefully lose. Later on I ask his whereabouts, since he is the father of a…

13 September 81

Half awake in the dream, I'm in a foxhole. VC sappers crawl past on my left. They have mortar tubes and begin shelling a position in front of me. I will move slowly, spring up and kill them. I shoot one. The other manages to slip away. He appears to be an FO[13]. He speaks quickly into a small radio handset, as if knowing he will die. We grapple. He stabs me several times. Then I kill him. The entire countryside goes up in flames. I don't know if I've done something good or bad.

I'm near the ocean. To survive the fire I must jump in the water. I swim forward, trying to beat the land, which also races ahead. A demon chases me. Though submerged, it's burning too. From behind, friendly forces shoot and kill it. Immediately all flames go out. I'm greeted by friendly voices. I'm welcomed back.

---

[13] FO (Forward Observer): a dangerous job usually held by an officer, who co-ordinated artillery and air strikes on enemy positions.

6 October 81

I'm in Africa with someone else. We're flying low, surveying the land. I see abandoned metal objects on the ground. We decide to salvage a damaged plane and tow it behind us. It's unclear which plane I'm flying. I steer, telling the other man I have little sense of control. He remains calm and patient. He gives me encouragement.

-There are no entries for the next 17 years-

22 August 98

I'm at a computer watching a documentary about Cambodia. There are several scenes of Phnom Penh. A man accompanies a female singer who relates her medical problems before regaining her voice.

I change the computer window. Live combat images appear on the screen. Helicopters wait to lift off. An American platoon chasing NVA run down a jungle slope covered by thick scrub. A GI throws a grenade. Now I'm with the platoon. The jungle has changed to short grass; the slope is edged on both sides by bamboo.

We begin taking rockets. I hear the whoosh, followed by the thud and crash. The rockets come closer. It's clear they're aiming at me. The enemy walks the rockets like mortars, missing by meters. Then I'm out in the open, trapped, every few seconds running back and forth. It's a child's game. Either I correctly dodge left or right, or be I'll killed. I'm not scared. I'm completely focused on survival.

I spot the NVA. They're launching rockets from behind a camouflaged wire fence. The rockets whiz past like giant .22 caliber bullets. I see my brother as if he were young. Angrily, I twice yell, "Get my M16 and ammo!" He does not run but walks toward my gear. Side stepping rockets, I yell again. Ignoring me, he ambles forward as if this were a joke.

15 February 99

Captain Plucinski, the battalion surgeon, places a slender nylon noose around my neck. Tethered to it is a loaded .45 pistol. He tells me to shoot myself. My fear turns to resistance. I will kill him instead. I probe the bottom of the grip; there's no magazine. I obtain a .38 pistol and shoot him in the head.

I'm walking my dog in a field. The field changes to heavy bush and triple canopy. Where is my dog? Is she lost? Then I'm in Vietnam and we kill enemy soldiers. The dead lie clumped in heaps, much like the ambush on 14 February 70. I imagine what it would be like for NVA to come across American dead.

21 February 99

I'm on another planet, caught up in a war, hiding in a cave. Attacking soldiers find me. The first one shoots me point blank; his rifle misfires. The second aims and shoots just as the atmosphere begins to freeze. It forms a protective shield in front of me. The bullet punctures the ice, then falls to the ground. The soldiers outside suffocate from lack of air. I'm next, but the dream changes.

A civilization on another planet is committing mass suicide. Soldiers have paired off in rows, separated one pair from the next by ten or fifteen meters. The distance between two soldiers is twenty or thirty meters. Armed soldiers advance against their unarmed partner. I'm not paired up, but caught in the fray and in danger of being shot.

22 February 99

I'm in a war. A plane of unknown origin flies overhead. It's identified as hostile and anti-aircraft guns open up. The plane circles in the cloudy sky; it begins to drop bombs. The sharp explosions create fountains of earth that shoot up and fall to the ground. There's a firestorm of smoke and flame. I run but get caught in the haze. I find a clearing. I find my dog.

11 March 99

I'm with Jamie Harter on a trail in Vietnam. We're on holiday. I tell him about war, about Chicom's and combat and death. We're both armed. I'm fearful of going out on ambush. I begin weeping, and sob deeply.

In 1994 the author met and worked with Dr. Jamie Harter and his wife, Dr. Sue Girod, at Southland Hospital, in Invercargill, New Zealand. By a strange coincidence, Drs. Harter and Girod were friends of Lt. Steve Sharp, who had become sheriff of their home town, Bloomington, Indiana. The author stayed at their spacious home, where the above dream occurred, when visiting Sheriff Sharp

12 March 99

I take the wrong bus to go to a dance and meet women, and instead go to a new movie about the Korean War. It's very crowded outside the theater. At the last moment I keep walking. I'm near a police station. In the distance I see a riot taking place. A group of people have broken one and two story windows; they're looting merchandise. I say nothing. The police finally take notice and storm the building.

With other people I watch the riot unfold. The rioters jump onto an electric scaffold and zoom up to the top floor. The police follow them into the building. Immediately, a girl jumps from the roof. We watch as she plummets down. I turn away at the last moment as she hits the pavement. When I look back, her head, likely split open, is covered by a sheet. A woman next to her is wailing. The body moves. She is still alive. She is moaning.

With someone else, I go inside the building. We believe the others have jumped from one rooftop to the next, making good their escape. In the basement there are large empty rooms. We walk up one or two flights, to old empty rooms made of rotted wood. A black man, an authority of some kind, sees us. We run. He confronts us later.

I'm in classroom. Bao Ninh is critiquing my work. He speaks perfect English. His voice is warm, yet powerful. He commends what is good, denotes what is flawed. He sounds very much like the poet Peter Kane Dufault. I'm learning a great deal. Ninh pauses to make a general remark. I mock him. Angered, he says he will not tolerate that sort of reply, hinting the class is over. I apologize twice, saying I will leave so the class can continue. I will come back the next day. I apologize again, but inwardly I'm still angry. Ninh seems to accept, but I'm forced to confront the conflicts of my nature, to understand them. The recognition is painful.

Both dreams occurred while visiting former Lt. Steve Sharp in Bloomington, Indiana.

Peter Kane Dufault was a WWII bomber pilot, activist, highly regarded musician and poet the author befriended in 1997. For many years he lived in a shack in the woods in Hillsdale, NY.

14 March 99

I'm with a group of Special Forces sol*diers in Vietnam. At close quarters we're attacked by NVA. One charges directly at us. He wears a gas mask and wields a chemical/biological weapon. A Special Forces soldier assaults him hand to hand.

The dream took place after the final visit with former lieutenant, then Sheriff Steve Sharp.

22 March 99

I’m on a rear base in Vietnam, sleeping outside a small bunker made of loose sand that is shored up on all sides. There is no barbed wire, there are no trips or claymores. It’s rumored the base will be attacked tonight. I go from one man to the next, asking where I can get an M16, ammo and magazines. I have nothing. A doctor reaches behind a wall and brings back a handful of plastic magazines made for toy guns.

The dream changes. I’m with a group of emotionally disturbed people. I’m lying on the cold floor. There’s a woman the others want me to meet, but I’m not interested in her. I’m giving up, regressing, curling up like an animal.

27 April 99

I'm in a snowy field. There is much chaos and confusion. Everything is blurred by thick swirling snow. Refugees wear thick clothing to keep warm. I'm trying to find the Americans. I walk to a woman I recognize. A reporter, she's calm. Panicked, I ask her, "Where are the Americans?" She points and says, "By the woman with the child." I run in the direction she's pointed toward but no one is there. Seated at a table, the same woman appears. She hands me three letters addressed to me. Each contains official or important documents. The letters have been opened and searched. I go back to the snowy field. A man and a woman trudge toward me. The man comes up close. Suddenly he points a long stick at me. I hesitate. He shoots. I fall and feel blood filling my chest. I feel the life force leaving me. I experience the process of dying. It's so ordinary. I'm not afraid. Just before death, I wake up.

2 June 99

I'm witness to the execution of the condemned at close range. They're shot by Asian men wearing military clothes. There is little movement or sound. No one struggles or attempts to escape. The shot is fired, the body falls.

8 June 99

In the present, I'm with someone else in Vietnam. We've gotten lost walking through swamp and terrain that borders a river. We pass an American who holds up a strand of fishing line with a lure attached to it. "This came all the way from Texas," he says. We continue walking. I say, "We're supposed to be going to An Loc or Loc Ninh." I take the lead, follow a path, a well-used trail, and emerge in a clearing. It's clean and well-tended; I'm reminded of Maplewood Park[18].

I'm in a trench in charge of an M-60 or SAW. Opposite me, less than ten yards away, in another trench, are several Americans. Lt. Sharp tells me to fire on them but I don't want to kill them. Waking up from the dream I'm half shouting, "Get down."

---

[18] Maplewood Park: known from childhood, a 25 acre semi-wooded park with trees, foot paths, footbridges, ball fields and playgrounds.

24 June 99

I'm struggling with a policeman who has caught me breaking into a car. He shoots me point blank, but it's only a flesh wound. I run. He shoots me twice in the chest. My blood spatters on a wall in front of me. I'm dying.

The dream occurred while attending the 12th Annual William Joiner Center Writer's Conference in Boston.

26 June 99

I'm in a small shack in the woods, terrified. Nearby, a machine gun roars. Raising up off the wood floor, I go to the screen window. My vision is blurred. I'm blind.

The dream occurred while attending the 12th Annual William Joiner Center Writer's Conference in Boston.

28 June 99

I'm with a group of people in danger. A seated black woman, who is light skinned, over and over repeats, "If ever I go... If ever I go..." She's unaware that she's dying. I take her in my arms to divert her attention. I imagine a man from behind will execute her. At the last moment I will say, "Never mind, shoot us both."

The dream occurred while attending the 12th Annual William Joiner Center Writer's Conference in Boston

23 July 99

In daylight, I'm with a group of people walking along a road or trail. It's as if we're refugees. A smelly old woman next to me has a bad heart. I don't want to be near her and move on. Finally, we arrive at our destination. I sit with a young boy at a picnic table; he's reading a thick book about war. He's reading the section on Vietnam. Together we look at the pictures. Several NVA, having dragged two dead GI's into the street, castrate them. Suddenly the image becomes real, and we're attacked. It's dark and difficult to see and they are over running our position. I hear screams and bullets, a grenade explodes close by. Moments later an NVA clears the berm and bayonets me.

18 August 99

With a black man I'm on a boat or the tip of an island, at war at sea. People are trying to kill us. I have several grenades strung together like a six pack of beer. I unhook one frag, then activate another by pushing the safety off, pulling the pin, then hurl the remaining grenades into the sea. My aim is short but effective. There is a huge underwater explosion followed by a whoosh and blast spout. We laugh and smile, knowing we've killed the enemy.

21 August 99

I'm in charge of a LRRP[22] squad made up of myself, Larry Johnson, Joe Dorio, and a good-looking girl. We walk through dull gloomy jungle. I have a crush on the girl. She ignores my advances, but does not push me away. A new man is sent out to replace or challenge my command. I shoot him in the leg. There is some kind of alert and I begin sorting through the ammo bandoliers. Larry or the girl says "Just hand them out." Then we are ambushed.

I'm up in a tree, drawing fire. I shoot back with my forty-five. The bullets are strong and powerful. I yell to Larry to throw a frag. I can see the NVA who are shooting at me. I yell to Larry and the girl that I will not die for nothing. I tell the girl I love her. Then I am shot.

---

[22] LRRP: Long Range Reconnaissance Patrol, a small Army Ranger team that patrols deep in enemy-held territory. LRRP patrols in Vietnam were extremely dangerous.

27 September 99

I'm with a group of excited soldiers in a foreign country, Israel or Palestine. We're in a large, open fortified area with many steps and rooms. Everyone is armed, waiting to assault or be attacked. I talk with the leader, a very important man, but can only obtain a .38 pistol and ammunition. I'm not afraid to go out like this.

1 January 2000

Since last entry I have experienced only one nightmare. Noteworthy is the development of emotional flooding with readiness towards weeping. I've spoken with the following men: Company commander Captain Leland Hyslop; company head medic Roy Abbott; third platoon leader Lieutenant Steve Sharp; point man Larry Roy; squad leader Jerry Bieck; fourth platoon squad leader Carl Lee (who, on LZ Ranch, cradled Mike Dawson in his arms before he died); second platoon squad leader Jackie McBride. I've visited RTO Mike Wilson in Michigan, and Lieutenant Steve Sharp in Indiana. I located the widow of Bill Williams, replying to her desperate letter twenty years after we wrote her from the jungle, telling her Bill was dead.

In summary, I have obtained modest relief from sleep disturbance, though I continue to lock the bedroom door, sleep with my back against the wall, and keep a well-honed machete within arms reach.

2 January 2000

It's dark and raining. I'm with a platoon of Israeli soldiers dressed like American grunts. Each man wears a poncho. We are climbing the rungs of a vertical tunnel. No one talks. We are going to war.

In farm country, I'm one of the last survivors of a group who've been starved, shot and burnt from their homes. Everywhere, decaying corpses rot in tall dry grass. We're waiting to die.

I talk with the opposing force. A young man, friendly, gifted in mathematics, offers to end the fighting by settling debts. He shows me how much we owe compared to what is owed us. His side has wealth from lottery winnings. Quick calculations reveal the debts are equal. I accept his offer, stating that I will tell the others if he does not kill me first.

19 January 2000

I'm at Pine Grove sleep away camp, preparing for war. Overhead, low flying jets fire rockets into the distance. We cheer as the missiles whoosh and spiral to their targets. We move out, juvenile soldiers, all less than fifteen. In a large field several teenage soldiers explode a device that releases a smoky fog that appears to be toxic. At detonation I'm hit by its shrapnel. I feel the cardboard splinters penetrate my back, but they do me no harm.

We march back to our starting point. I'm walking uphill on the wide trail which leads from the lake to the bunkhouses, weary from the weight of my pack. I walk next to an out of shape youngster. He huffs and puffs. In his hand he carries a silver-plated toy luger.

In addition to an M16, three bandoleers of ammo, and frags, the author carried a silver plated .45 pistol, given to him by a rear echelon staff sergeant, who could not believe that infantry medic's carried weapons.

10 March 2000

In a crowded street in Vietnam I'm a witness to war at close range. The first thing I see is an AK-47, stuck into a wall by its bayonet. There are angry words written on its stock. All around, Vietnamese men are frantically fighting, firing their M16s over a wall.

Next, I'm lying on a bunk bed, sorting through someone's belongings. This person, apparently dead, had collected stamps. Paging through a small album, I see many American air mail stamps I recall from my youth. Suddenly a man nearby is shot and falls. I see the bullets kick up dirt near him. Two nurses, wearing red and white striped dresses, come to his aid. Completely vulnerable, they turn their backs to the enemy. I'm amazed at their bravery, or foolishness. One nurse, in particular, comforts the man, who is mortally wounded.

4 April 2000

I'm in Cambodia, at the ambush site where the others threw themselves on me just before the second Chicom[24] exploded. In the dream, instead of guns chattering or the short snap of the Chicom's fuse, both sides scream and shout, preparing to rush forward in hand-to-hand combat. The NVA come at me with bayonets drawn. I don't resist, or fight, but cower and steel myself for the killing thrust. They prod me in the sides once or twice. Then, before death or capture, I wake up, the word *surrender* fresh in my mind.

---

[24] Chicom - see note page 13

13 April 2000

A man is lost at sea. I help to rescue him.

There is war. I'm hit in the back with shrapnel. Bao Ninh tends to me in hospital. He is clearly in charge of himself and the matter at hand. Like a Zen master, he is deliberate and clear in his actions. I complain and grow anxious, become uncooperative. Ninh ignores or engages me depending on my awareness of what is correct. At one point he appears to give up.

28 August 2000

In Vietnam, I'm a pilot in a helicopter that has crashed. Either the low altitude, or the jungle canopy enables a soft landing. There's little damage, but my co-pilot is slightly injured. There are only three or four grunts on board. I give them an order to form a perimeter but they do not obey. We're spotted by friendly civilians, and again, my orders are disobeyed. This happens a second time.

I'm a civilian on my way to work in the dark on a road crowded with pedestrians. People begin to sit by the roadside; something has happened. I search for a friendly or familiar face to inquire what's going on, then sit on a bench next to an older European man. He tells me a plane has crashed over an airport and that all flights have been canceled.

I look up and see many helicopters. It's like an enormous combat assault[25]. I board a small Loach[26] though it's not taking passengers. I'm loaded with combat gear. We fly as part of the combat assault and land on a base. There is no combat, but it's not clear when and where we should go. An Asian man directs me down steps to an empty high school lab. I throw down my gear and try to sleep on a lawn outside. I'm woken by a solider tugging my arm. He's upset over something I have caused. It's not serious and the soldier is not angry, only concerned.

I'm one of several white people caught up in a large group of black people who treat us well but who intend to kill us.

---

[25] combat assault: a formation of helicopters carrying combat troops flying toward a drop off zone

[26] Loach: a small helicopter used for observation

I'm with a woman who is either my daughter or my wife. Depressed and stoop shouldered, she's un-insightful, quiet and stubborn. We're running, being herded up steps and hallways. At one point there is a chance to escape. The woman hesitates. I tell her to follow me or let go my hand. I break free and run down a stairwell that leads to an Asian man with a mop and bucket. The area is fenced off. I implore him to let me pass. He's friendly but suspicious, but tells me where to go and what to avoid.

5 September 2000

I'm with a group of submariners out in the country. They seem to be a mix of Americans and Russians. The group has been detected and seeks to escape. I climb on top of the submarine, which rests on dry land. The captain, a Russian, stands beneath me. I steer the ship like a car down a long dirt road. We're spotted by Russian agents disguised as civilians. Soon we're chased by men who want to arrest us. I drive faster and faster and seem to have lost them. Then, because I've driven into a cul-de-sac, we must exit the submarine. Now it's every man for himself.

I try hiding in a barn cellar. Not quick enough, I'm caught. The captain is caught too. Then I escape, and run and find a woman sitting outside her house. I ask her for help but she refuses. I keep running. I have freedom now, but I'm at the edge of the sea. Large sand dunes reach into the clear water. I'm being pursued again and have no choice: I have to swim into the ocean. The water is warm and clear, the waves are big but not dangerous. It's very light and sunny. I try to escape by swimming underwater, but close at hand, three Russian agents triangulate my position. Beneath me, I see a large dark American submarine that has come to my rescue. It begins to rise from below, but too late. The agents begin shooting with pistols and high powered rifles. I am shot.

I'm in Ivy Hill Park, where I spent much of my childhood, near the tennis courts. Mike the RTO is with me. Above the tall trees a commercial plane veers low and loud; the left wing hits the tree tops and ignites. The plane spins and tumbles in the air, then crashes. I'm directly in its path and move just in time to avoid being killed by large pieces of bouncing wreckage. A capsule-like pod nearly crushes me, but I duck out of the way. The capsule is on fire; the pilots inside are trapped. The escape hatches are white hot, but from inside, or with my help, they're opened. I yell to the pilots, "Reach in and drag them out." We're all afraid the fuel tanks will explode. Then we are safe. Two pilots survive; one is dead.

26 September 2000

With two other men I'm in Ivy Hill Park at the center of a big parched field. Suddenly mortars begin to drop. I'm terrified. "They're walking them in," I shout. The shells fall in a neat vertical line, closing on our position. Swirling, low-hugging clouds erupt where the shells explode. We run up field. I turn around and see a dark brown wild horse caught in the bombardment. It escapes with few or no injuries from shrapnel. Then a black man, handsome and confident, appears down field. He swings a golf club in our direction. I recover the irregular shaped red ball, throwing it back with unexpected precision. He catches the ball on one sharp bounce and thanks me.

7 October 2000

I'm on a mission with a LRRP team. I've grown close to these men, especially the leader, and the man second in charge. In the morning, before moving out, I begin getting dressed, but the LRRPs leave without me. I'm angry and struggle with either catching up or turning back. I return to the rear and ask about the team. The leader and second in charge have been killed in an ambush. A survivor, dressed in civilian clothes, tells me the news in simple, almost cheerful terms, as if he were familiar with death in manner I'm not. Still, I'm overcome with emotion. Not with guilt, but with the impossible loss of irreplaceable men at the height of their youth.

8 October 2000

I'm in my Bronx apartment, sleeping. There's a noise in the foyer. Two dolls, hanging from a doorknob, have come to life. I speak to the male and female doll and feel happy. I've made two friends. Then we're outside in a country at war. The terrain is hilly and partially wooded. Helicopters fire rockets, which do not fully explode. Instead, on impact the force of the blast shoots out to the left and right. This happens several times.

We start running. A fighter plane appears overhead. I expect it to strafe us, but it pulls up from the power dive and, on the upswing, drops a cloud of white powder or gas. As we run, we're spotted or captured by police.

9 October 2000

I'm caught up in the violence in the Middle East and I am suffering a punishment. The Palestinians are clawing and tearing at each other, ripping themselves apart. I'm not in the direct fighting, though hundreds of men, somehow far, yet close and reduced in size, crawl over my feet and legs like ants, biting me as they fight between themselves. Periodically, an official, Israeli or Palestinian, asks me to write, hinting this will set me free. He asks the time. My mother is present and answers. Then I do, and correct her. The man becomes hostile towards me but I do not accept the offer to write.

17 October 2000

I'm on patrol with an American. We set up a perimeter and ambush site. We're in the jungle, which is in fact a large civilian park. I ask the other man for my M16 because I can't find it, but it's lost. He gives me my .45; he has the machine gun. In the morning, after an uneventful night, we head back to a car which will take us away. The car has been broken into. Items have been stolen. No one can be trusted.

I'm in domestic setting. A large powerful tiger eyes and tracks a furry pet cat. The cat tries to dodge and escape the tiger's playful swipes. Eventually the cat runs up a tree but the tiger easily follows it. The cat can't escape. On the ground it shows no fear and continues to rebuff the tiger.

Principles of life are explained to me by John or someone like him. I'm told to think of life as a daily game, to imagine luck or good fortune. I agree, but question why this works, since it does.

11 November 2000

I'm in Vietnam with the combat vets from last night's group. They're talking too loud; I'm anxious they'll give away our position. We recon a small abandoned ville and examine an old foundation. Next, I'm in a hospital corridor, walking with Steve, a squad leader from my old platoon. He's been shot badly in the thigh. As we walk a doctor points out the injury, which is bandaged and bleeding.

Prior to a symposium on war, the evening was spent with prominent writer's, among them American and Vietnamese combat vets, nearly all of whom told obscene jokes and laughed uproariously.

26 November 2000

We're in the jungle on patrol. I'm speaking with Ray, the RTO for the command platoon. In the dream he's young and trim, but his features are gaunt, weary, hollowed out. The terrain is like Song Be[28], but the scrub and bush are sparse, offering less cover. Ray's eyes are full of fear and foreboding.

I'm in a wealthy environment, similar to Klinic am Zurichberg[29]. My family is present. Most prominent is my grandmother, who remains repressive and remote.

[28] Song Be: a province in Vietnam

[29] Klinic am Zurichberg: a Swiss mental institution where the author resided for two months in 1977

1 January 2001

I'm in a familiar house. My brother and I are young. He throws a heavy silver ring at me. I chase him, but he hides and disappears. I enter a bedroom but find only a rumpled blanket under the bed. Then I spot him through the frosted glass of a bathroom window.

My brother says, "I guess I should come out." I agree and confront him with the ring, which I have found. Very sternly I say, "If you ever treat me with disrespect again, I'll kill you."

We're playing in a desert-like setting. My brother asks if I meant what I said. I'm angry and want an excuse to be violent. My brother says, "You wouldn't shoot me." I tell him to be quiet. He continues speaking. I shoot him point-blank in the head and he falls down dead. He looks to be ten or twelve years old. I'm older. Eighteen or nineteen.

14 January 2001

I'm in the country with my dog, Rusty. As usual, she's off the leash. I'm reading a war story. It ends by telling how men, desperate for cover, would dive down in the latrine area, only to be stained with shit. Just as I read this, my hand is stained from shit streaked on the ground. I wash it off in a large pool of fresh clear water. The dog swims in the water. She's happy, though nervous and high-strung, which was her nature.

We continue and arrive at a wealthy residential area. It's safe and quiet; there are many plants and trees. I wear blue jeans and walk with confidence. The dog, as was her way, romps and sprints ahead. We arrive at a store, which is closed. The dog jumps up on a small landing. I pet her; she places her arm on mine and nuzzles me. The dog and I share a profound sense of happiness and well-being. It's the deepest sense of love I've felt in a long time. Then a young married couple stop to ogle and pet the dog and the spell is broken. We continue walking, and it's good, but the intense feeling of love is gone.

While on a three day Stand Down in Bien Hoa, the author called home from a MARS station (military/ham radio patch to commercial phone), repeatedly asking about the dog. In 1980, when the dog was hit by a car, my mother did not call me, a long standing request if the dog was injured or sick. Instead, she notified the city's Animal Control, which sent out a truck, which picked up and disposed of the corpse. I located the truck driver, who related the dog had been thrown on a heap. I was unable to retrieve and bury it. The loss and rage were enormous.

16 January 2001

I'm with a group of young soldiers under fire. Some are new, others have seen combat. The terrain is semi-desert and mountainous. I obtain an M-79 and shoot it. The shell streaks through the night; far away it explodes in a ball of flame. The RTO speaks without having to break squelch. Apparently the radio operates by voice recognition. The RTO is frightened, he's trying to locate the other troops, but can't see them. I need more ammo but can't find it.

I'm high up in a tree with two small children. Opposite us we watch a mother bird feed her young. She flees at the approach of a giant rat, which enters the nest and hunts for food. The rat slithers down the tree, with the dead body of an animal hanging from its mouth. Then the rat starts climbing up the tree. The children are frightened. I plan to let the rat crawl near, then punch the glass collar that it must pass through to reach us. When the rat's head is beneath the glass I begin punching it, ignoring possible injury of my fist. The glass breaks; blood from the rat's smashed head streams down the tree trunk. The rat falls and dies.

It's night. Gloria Emerson knocks on my door to wake me. I get dressed. I'm young and handsome and brush my hair in a brash, swept back manner. We're headed to school. I'm wearing jeans. I've slung a towel over my bare chest. I turn back to put a shirt on. Later, Gloria gives me the title page from a faded manuscript of poetry. She signs it but makes an error, which she crosses out and signs again.

With someone else, I'm on a great snowy white mountain.

The previous day, the author had spoken to and planned to visit noted author and war correspondent Gloria Emerson.

Two powerful trained horses run down the mountain as if it was an obstacle course. They do tricks. They endure hardship. At the unexpected, they do not hesitate, but immediately improvise.

24 January 2001

I'm at war. The terrain is rocky and dry. We're being mortared. The shells fall close by. A man who resembles Ray the RTO[32] is struck by the blast of a near direct hit. The instant he's killed his body seizes up, as if he were struck dumb. There's no blood, no sign of injury. A second man is killed the same way. No one moves. I run for cover.

I'm a guest renting a room in a residential area filled with many large wood houses. The people here are friendly. I'm skateboarding down a narrow sidewalk, propelling the board by clenching my toes or pushing down hard. A block away a tree catches fire. A fierce wind whips the fire out of control. The sky turns white from the heat and flames. It seems the house with my belongings will catch fire.

No one panics. I rush into the house to recover my back pack. I'm confused. Which room is mine? I find it in another room. It's large and half open to the elements. On the way out I watch a good-looking middle-aged woman undress. It's very erotic.

Outside, things are calm. I meet a young man, a veterinarian. His dog has burns on its back. The dog is aware of its injury but remains feisty. Somewhat humorously I say to the doctor, "So, you have casualties." I can't recall his words, but he is optimistic.

[32] CP RTO: command platoon radio telephone operator

4 February 2001

I'm with a large black woman who resembles the poet Marilyn Nelson[33]. We're sitting in the office of Peter Ahr. She listens while I speak about war. Suddenly a low resonant howl escapes me. The black woman says, "I know what that is." I begin weeping.

---

[33] Marilyn Nelson: noted poet met at the 12th Annual William Joiner Center Writer's Workshop in 2001

7 February 2001

On a cancer ward all the patients are men. One complains that his nose is too large. Another declares that without his doctor he would have died, but has lived an extra two years. The ward is home-like. The doctors are friendly. Each has his own cure; some succeed, others fail. My doctor is a woman. She is dedicated and loving.

A staff member and I reach a doctor's office at the same time. I push the door open; it's immediately slammed shut, catching my finger. The staff member knocks and is let in. I leave, aware that protocol must be obeyed.

I become frustrated and rebel. For punishment I'm sent to a large forest to gather pine needles in long neat rows. After several hours on my hands and knees I try to escape. Using a dog, my doctor captures me. I quit the ward. In her presence I get dressed. I'll be traveling heavy–there are my two backpacks, a toothbrush too small for my mouth. My doctor tries to discourage me, but I'm angry and sad. On the wall hangs a photograph of a male doctor at war. His pants are torn and dirty. His knees are wounded; he's running for help. I say, "What does he know? I was the medic. They all came to me." I begin weeping.

1 June 2001

I'm sent to my old platoon without medical supplies, my pack, my weapon or ammo. We patrol thick jungle much like Song Be. In a clearing I carry the M-79 over my shoulder, but it's awkward and doesn't feel right. I'm angry.

We pass another patrol. They've captured a POW who is larger than life. We enter a large school, where I become lost. I speak with a young woman who refers me to a man who listens to my story, which I relate in anger. He says I should not be mad at him, he's a CO, a conscientious objector. He asks if I understand the term. I tell him, "No." I tell him I'm politically and morally ignorant. I tell him I'm worried about my men. Who will help if they are hit? I tell him, "Look, I have the Combat Medic Badge, the Silver Star, two Bronze Stars for Valor, the Air Medal, the Army Commendation Medal, so I know about war and all I want is the right equipment and to be with my men."

2 July 2001

I'm in a large room at ground level. Its green walls and floors are made from smoothed out earth. Large square windows without glass overlook a forbidding no-man's-land. The NVA begin shooting. I return fire. They're everywhere. Several NVA reach inside. I push them off and continue shooting. They're everywhere, but I'm not afraid. I keep fighting. There is no escape.

25 July 2001

I'm brought back to Vietnam. The platoon tells me I look good. I'm wearing my old jungle fatigues and steel helmet. I have no gear, no leech straps beneath my knees. I want to tell them that dressed like this, ordinary people think I'm strange, but I keep silent.

With Mike Wilson and Bill Williams I walk to the water point. We pass through a small town, then into a forest where I become lost. I walk to a highway, then pass through a circle of college students. I expect unkind remarks, but the students are friendly. At a busy intersection a college professor smiles. "Where is the water?" I ask. He tells me. I find a dark, turbulent river. This can't be the water point, though I know it is.

Frustrated, I sleep under a moonlit canopy of thick brush. I wake up under a large plastic tarp. Crawling forward I accidentally wake the squad leader, Steve Melhop. I say, "It's me, Doc." He throws me a pair of bowling shoes which are too small. A man I have never seen glares at me with contempt, then throws me a pair that fit. Then everyone leaves. I look out from beneath the tarp. Someone inside a nearby house appears in silhouette, then vanishes. I anticipate an ambush. I imagine being shot in the head. I imagine how

---

Bill Williams, from Hailey, Idaho, was a college graduate, killed in Cambodia on 3June 70. Wounded while an infantryman in another division, which resulted in a hearing loss, he was re-assigned to a rear job writing casualty reports. With two months left in his tour, for refusing to lower the American casualty rates and increase the NVA/VC body count, Sergeant Williams was punitively transferred to D 1/7 First Cavalry. In 1994 the author contacted his next-of-kin, who related that for twenty-five years the Army refused to explain the reason Bill was sent back into combat, or the manner in which he died. In fact, he had been shot in the head. My last words to him, before the medivac took him away were, "Bill, this is Doc. Everyone loves you." He died three days later.

Steve will comfort me. It's raining. I have no water, ammo, or weapon.

14 September 2001

I'm with my old platoon on LZ Ranch in Cambodia. We're pressed up against the berm. An attack is coming. My M16 is broken. There's no trigger or clip. A sergeant offers me his weapon, but I refuse, saying he is the better grunt.

I help to invent a catapult that hurls a half dozen grenades at a time. However, the device is faulty. Ed the point man uses it to initiate the attack.

The scene changes. We're in a village. An old VC hides in a hut hoping to escape. I throw him down and sit on him. He's taken prisoner, but will not speak. I devise a way to torture him. We dig a vertical hole, bury him up to his neck, then place a clear plastic bag cover over his head. We will urinate on him. But the VC is stubborn and stays silent. He accepts that he will die.

We hear shooting and run for cover. I find a Viet Cong who resembles David Boyle, my best college friend. He's trying to steal American weapons from a display case, but instead, grabs an umbrella. I tell him to give up. When he refuses, we fight. Each time I stab his belly he says, "Kill me." I feel terrible. It's as if I knew this man. When he weakens, I take him in my arms and call for help. His stomach leaks on me. I'm crying. I'm saying, "Oh God.... Oh God." American soldiers arrive. They look perplexed, awed. We march to a hospital.

3 November 2001

In the present I'm with Bao Ninh in Vietnam. He leads me around, showing me the different sites and soldiers. There's a certain intimacy, a certain understanding between us all. We communicate without language. At a rehab center, I sit with a Vietnamese vet who sketches pencil drawings. When he sharpens the point by pressing it into the stub of his lower arm, I wince, and offer to help, but he declines. He's proud and self-sufficient; this is how he does things. In another room I see drawings made by school children. They're colorful, lively, happy. There is no sense of war. I wake up thinking I must contact Bao Ninh. I must thank him for giving me hope.

2 December 2001

I'm with the platoon on patrol in Antarctica. Men with foot problems are asked to go on sick call. Nearly all are lame, but march to the aid station in the cold, hard snow. They overwhelm the staff ,who make complaints against them. I'm sad because no one cares, no one understands how we suffer. A kind, middle-aged black medic tells me that Larry Roy, our point man, whose bad feet should have kept him out of the Army, will go home. But when I speak to Larry, he says he's been denied sick call. He's seen no one.

4 January 2002

It's dark. I'm with the platoon in a foreign country. We're on an exposed slope facing the wood line. A voice mocks us. I'm trying to invent a weapon that will fire small grenades more accurately than tossing them. The clumsy firing device resembles a flintlock. Only the first grenade explodes in the wood line. Nearby, Ed Torres, the point man, quickly chucks grenades one after another. The platoon retreats. I become separated, lose my weapon, and panic. Then we regroup and fall back.

An old officer says my boonie hat is worn out. The flimsy material has lost its shape. My CMB[35], pinned in front, is missing, as are the encircling love beads, the Cav patch sewn on top, the grenade rings clipped to the brim. There is no ground-in muck, no accumulated dirt and sweat. This hat cannot be mine. We enter a large wooden house and line up in a stairwell, which leads to a cellar where the men will be issued new hats. A pretty American girl with long hair makes her way past. I have no desire for her. It's a good feeling to be with my men.

[35] CMB: Combat Medic Badge

1 July 2002

I'm in Europe. There is my old platoon, young, full-haired, smiling. They welcome me, then complain. It's a bad area. One out of six will die of prostate cancer. It's in the water, which spills over large brick buildings; it's in the ground.

A young soldier shows me a gem bought from a villager. He regards its beauty and power but I can tell it's fake. The villager, who is middle-aged and wears a business suit, leaves his house. He walks toward me. I throw the gem in his face. "What are you doing?" I say. "This is uranium." Aloof and calm, he curls his hand around my neck, then releases it. We return to his house. There is the long flight home. I begin planning my escape.

9 July 2002

I'm on a combat assault. A few of us ride in the chopper. The rest stand on the slicks. We carry full combat gear: pack, weapon, helmet, ammo.

We fly toward the Ivy Hill Apartments. From high up I see buildings, which look like photographs. We land on a rooftop. I see my brother. At the same time I see a horrible sight and walk toward it. The intact body of an American soldier glows like fireplace embers. His internal organs, hardened to stone, are fully visible. I shout to my brother, "How did this happen?" He says he doesn't know. I'm standing over the corpse. I can tell my brother is lying.

19 August 2002

I'm driving a jeep in the country. The land is green and dotted with old wooden houses. I park near Doug Anderson[36] and his friend. We begin talking. I hear chopper blades and look up. A Huey with Red Cross markings prepares to land close by. I say to Doug, "Oh God, it's a medivac." The scene changes. I'm in a bar crowded with soldiers. I recognize several men, though I mistake one man for someone else. I take a long swig from a bottle. I'm crying. I want the men to see this. I want the man mistaken for someone else to see this.

---

[36] Doug Anderson: Marine Corp Vietnam veteran, noted poet and author, met at the 12th Annual William Joiner Center Writer's Conference in 2001

24 October 2002

I'm searching for NVA hidden in the stalls of public bathrooms. In a frenzy I kick open the doors. The enemy wear green uniforms and have long black hair. They are silent and beaten and offer no defense. I'm yelling as I shoot. I'm screaming. I'm shooting at close range. When the dead slump down, there is little blood. After the killing I shoot them again.

26 November 2002

It's the present day. In a large flat field I watch as prisoners are beaten senseless by the CIA. The victims are dragged off and thrown into piles, condemned to be shot. The bloodied, half-conscious men plead for their lives. The cruel agents ignore them. Then it's my turn. I beg not to be killed, but the process begins.

11 December 2002

I'm with a large group of noisy veterans in a crowded restaurant. A menacing black man approaches. We argue. Point blank, he starts shooting me in the hip with a forty-five automatic, taunting me with every shot. I'm screaming, "Stop it! Stop it!" Then I give up. He's right. I'm wrong. I sense the bullets have missed my vital organs and that I will live. The next day I return with Ed Torres, who is dressed in full combat gear. I find the black man. With a small pair of scissors I quickly stab each of his lungs twice, then puncture his heart. The skin of his chest fills with blood. "I'm sorry," I say, mocking him. "I'm so very, very sorry." I continue taunting him until he is dead.

25 December 2002

I'm at a dance with an attractive woman who has promised me a place to live. We're just friends. After the dance we walk down a snowy moonlit street. We are happy and young. She puts her arm around my shoulder. "I like you," she says. "I really like you." Then we sit in her car and neck. Our kisses are sensual, giving, tender. She removes her blouse and straddles me. Outside, a small wooden sign is tacked to a street lamp. Its handwritten letters state, "Kit Karson Scouts[37]." I raise up and embrace her. "That's gold," I say. "Absolute gold." Then we make love.

---

[37] Kit Karson Scouts captured NVA or VC who were retrained to work with American infantry.

9 October 2008

My brother and I are in the jungle. I'm not a medic but an RTO. My brother is new to Vietnam. I'm breaking him in. I receive a message from a pilot flying an OV 10 Bronco, a lightly armed reconnaissance plane. The pilot names a mechanical part that he needs. I take out a pen, spread a napkin on the ground, and tell my brother to hold it flat while I write it down. My brother laughs at me. I take out my forty-five pistol. I say, "If you do that again, I'll kill you." My brother laughs. I shoot him point blank in the chest. I wake up saying, "You didn't listen so I killed you."

The mail for this day included a package from my brother, which contained the anti-war film Living With War, a documentary based on the Crosby Stills & Nash concerts of 2006. At the film's beginning, war journalist Mike Cerre is introduced. Embedded with the Marines during the invasion of Iraq, in Vietnam he flew an OV 10.

Articles of Possible Interest Concerning
The Scientific Value of Dream Journals

Domhoff, G. W. (2015). Dreaming as embodied simulation: A widower dreams of his deceased wife. Dreaming, 25, 232-256. http://www2.ucsc.edu/dreams/Library/domhoff_2015.html

Domhoff, G. W. & Schneider, A. (2008). Studying dream content using the archive and search engine on DreamBank.net. Consciousness and Cognition, 17, 1238-1247. http://www2.ucsc.edu/dreams/Library/domhoff_2008c.html.

Marc Levy served as an infantry medic with Delta Company, First Battalion, Seventh Cavalry in Vietnam and Cambodia in 1970. His decorations include the Combat Medic Badge, Silver Star, two Bronze Stars with V, Air Medal and ArCom. His war related prose and poetry have been widely published. His website is MedicInTheGreenTime.com. His email address is silverspartan@gmail.com.

www.ingramcontent.com/pod-product-compliance
Lightning Source LLC
Chambersburg PA
CBHW020918090426
42736CB00008B/686

* 9 7 8 0 6 9 2 7 7 6 3 7 7 *